SORRY CHARLIE!

Donald Gorbach

ISBN-10 1981541748
ISBN-13 978-1981541744

"THE GREAT REGRET OF MY LIFE
IS THAT I DIDN'T HAVE CHILDREN."

— CHARLIE ROSE
(I GUESS HE MIGHT WANT TO REVISIT THIS!)

REALITYCOVERBOOKS.COM